Activate your Home or Office

For Success in

Relationships and Collaboration

With Feng Shui

Published by Termina Feng Shui

Queensland, Australia

Copyright © 2016 Termina Feng Shui. All rights reserved. No part of this book may be reproduced or transmitted in any form without written permission from the authors and publisher, except for brief inclusion of quotations or for review purposes. First Edition

This book is designed to provide competent and reliable information regarding the subject matter covered. However, it is sold with the understanding that the author and publisher are not engaged in rendering legal, financial, or other professional advice. Laws vary from country to country and if legal or other assistance is required, the services of a professional should be sought. The intent of the author is only to offer information of a general nature to help you in your quest for well-being, the author and the publisher assume no responsibility for your actions. The author shall have no liability or responsibility to any person or entity regarding physical, psychological, emotional, financial, commercial damages, special, incidental, or consequential by the information contained in this book.

Activate your Home or Office For in Relationships and Collaboration

Contents

Introduction
What is Feng Shui
Invite your desired relationships in
Clutter management
Activate your relationships and collaboration
- Personal Intimate Relationship
- Family Relationships
- Family Collaboration
- Relationships with Children and Grandchildren
- Motherhood and Compassion
- Empowerment/Self-Empowerment
- General Supportive Luck
- The Trinity of Luck
- General Collaboration
- Enhance Your Connection to Heaven
- Business Collaboration
- Education Collaboration

Relationship and collaboration enhancers
- CLARITY
- CELEBRATION
- HONESTY and HONOUR
- PURITY
- JOY
- TRANSPARENCY
- FAITH
- TRANSFORMATION
- TENDERNESS

General and quick tips
- Dining Room

- Bedroom
- Bathroom
- Front Door
- Cleansing
- General

Create a vision Board

Introduction

Create the love and collaboration you want in your relationships. Have closer and harmonious relationship with your significant other, attract your ideal partner, have more friends, have better relationships with your children or your family, have better relationships with your work or business colleagues, be more outgoing, be more open to others, see the value in yourself and appreciate YOU. Feng Shui principles open the flow of Qi for the relationships and happiness you desire in your life.

The important thing to remember is that your environment is your physical visualisation board and this unconsciously creates your outcomes, 24 hours a day, 7 days a week. The Chinese and now quantum physics teach us that we are surrounded by energy, in fact, everything is energy. Our environment is energy. Einstein told us this *"Everything is energy and that's all there is to it. Match the frequency of the reality you want and you cannot help but get that reality. It can be no other way. This is not philosophy. This is physics."* Energy or energy forces in Feng Shui are termed as Qi (chi). A good flow energy, also known as frequency, leads to abundance, prosperity and happiness while negative energy leads to misfortune and unhappiness.

Whether you are Building, Designing, Buying, Renting, Selling, Living or Working in a premises, Feng Shui improves your life in so many ways. If there is something going on in your life that you wish to change or improve: Health, career, relationships, financial issues, support, business, wealth, or academic achievement. — You name it — it's all possible by adjusting your environment. All of life circumstances fall under the Feng Shui umbrella of possibilities and there is no limit to what you can improve or amplify positively when these ancient principles and science is applied.

With Feng Shui we can arrange our environment so that we receive maximum support with solutions for improvement, maximising the energy of the home or office for the occupants so that there is improvement in the health, wealth and relationship areas of their lives. The 4000 year old art and science of Feng Shui helps harness the power of good energy in the home and cures the effects of negative energy. Many home and business owners confirm to the fact that Feng Shui has helped them with their struggles and even result in a more attractive living or work space.

What is Feng Shui

Feng Shui is a science and ancient art based on laws that govern the flow of energy. The term Feng Shui translates to "wind-water" in English and is a Chinese Metaphysic Art, practised through formulas and calculations using energy forces referred to as Qi (chi). Both Feng and Shui are associated with good health and prosperity which is why the art is so highly regarded in the east. Energy in the environment remains stuck, people are prevented from moving forward, or experience unwanted circumstances, however, by increasing the flow of energy this clears the path to propel forward and to bring to fruition desired intentions. By creating Positive changes in the environment it produces improvements in the level and flow of Qi energy bringing high levels of good fortune and creating a more favourable and harmonious layout for a home or office.

Today Feng Shui is used widely around the world, seeing value in what the Chinese have known for years and the objectives vary depending on the home or business owners desired outcome. The common desired outcomes include; healthy family relationships, improved physical and mental health, preservation or growth of financial wealth and harmony. When we consider the energy we put out and take in, and apply the Feng Shui principles, we discover that we have more control over our lives than we originally believed. Feng Shui is our opportunity to direct the flow of energy in our lives as we choose. For those of you looking for a way to bring more successful relationships into your life, you can use the basics of Feng Shui to help you achieve your goal.

This book contains tips provided in a manner through harnessing the positive energies that you and your property can receive through the use of Feng Shui principles.

Invite your desired relationships in

Feng Shui is a science that works beyond the physical world of cause and effect, operating on an energetic level to bring you the highest levels of good fortune. Using Feng Shui principles you create a better flow of energy in your environment and consciously direct that flow to achieve the relationships you desire in your life.

The positive energy of an environment surrounds you and influences you 24 hours a day, seven days a week, your whole lifetime, this also applies to uncured negative energy. Feng Shui is like a form of acupuncture or bar codes for the unified field of energy that includes your home and body. Activate or cure areas within your home or workspace and you start a flow of energy through your body, mind, and soul for more success in your career, health, relationships and growth.

Brain Waves - Your home or workspace is a living, vibrating energy in a vast unified field of energy. Everything in a home influences the flow of active and passive energy also known as positive or negative Qi. This energy wave of flow is similar to the brainwaves formed from your own thinking process. The outcomes in your life are results of brain waves you habitually create with your thoughts. And the outcomes you experience in life are either suppressed or enhanced by the energy fields or environmental brainwaves emitting in your physical surroundings.

There are two brainwave energy fields or environmental brainwaves are beta and alpha frequencies. Beta frequencies reflect chaos and are present in cluttered rooms, drab, dirty spaces, environments with no cosiness or spaces filled with depressing or violent images, dead flowers and piles of papers. This environment feels overwhelming and joyless. It produces victim mentality where one feels unsupported. It creates the feeling of struggling uphill. In this state it is very hard to create what you want toward a better life. However, when you begin to declutter and clean the spaces. Introduce colours and uplifting images, the beta energy wave's shift to bring in the flow of alpha brainwaves. You invite in new opportunities and attract more of the power available to you. This positive flow brings to you good fortune in your career, relationships, health and growth as well as feeling more empowered.

Feng Shui has shown through the centuries that improving your success is within your control. When you change or add other things such as colours or items or position yourself or your furniture, this creates a positive spiralling of energy upward that affects your good fortune and you are in a much better position to attract what you desire. When you decide what you want or to make a change in your life the first thing you must do is get rid of the old to make room for the new. If you want certain relationships, you must make room, change or add something to invite it in.

General Space Feng Shui is universal. Each of the eight compass directions, plus the center direction, is associated with a specific life area, element, number, shape, material, colour, and symbol. Some of the directions include a representative season and animal. Any area can be activated by placing specific elements, colours, items or images, in the specific compass direction and area of your home or workplace.

Compass directions for Relationships and Collaboration, including Relationship with yourself are north for clarity and self-empowerment. South for passion and celebration. East for honesty, family relationships and collaboration. West for transparency, joy and relationships with children or grandchildren. Northwest for, general supportive luck, transformation, faith and Business Collaboration. Northeast for education collaboration. Southwest for Romantic luck, tenderness, general collaboration, motherhood, compassion, as well as business collaboration. Southeast for forgiveness and release.

Decluttering and cleaning is the start in creating a flow of positive Qi. By placing items and images you activate environmental affirmations that represent what it is you want to have happen in this area of your life. These environmental affirmations are your physical visualisation board. Every time you look at your items or objects you are sending the Qi in this direction, consciously and unconsciously.

Feng Shui for love, relationships and marriage harmony is one of the most popular applications. However, before you activate these to attract love, collaboration or a possible long term relationship/marriage you must love and appreciate yourself, practice the energy of self-love.

Create a new energy you need to manifest your intentions. Have faith, love and know that each of us are wonderful, any beliefs, fears or judgements are only influences from the environments we grew up in. Here is a quote from *Marianne Williamson, A Return to Love*, *"Our deepest fear is not that we are inadequate. Our deepest fear is that we are powerful beyond measure. It is our light, not our darkness that most frightens us. We ask ourselves, 'Who am I to be brilliant, gorgeous, talented, fabulous?' Actually, who are you not to be? You are a child of God. Your playing small does not serve the world. There is nothing enlightened about shrinking so that other people won't feel insecure around you. We are all meant to shine, as children do. We were born to make manifest the glory of God that is within us. It's not just in some of us; it's in everyone. And as we let our own light shine, we unconsciously give other people permission to do the same. As we are liberated from our own fear, our presence automatically liberates others."*

- For joyful love, collaboration and relationships, be sure to create spaces that reflects the beauty of the relationship you want to be in. Love and appreciate yourself.

- Surround yourself with images of people who give you loving support and encourage you to be yourself.

- For intimate relationships place objects or images in groups of twos, for example, two birds or two hearts. Only allow objects and images you love and remove anything you do not love.

Clutter management

Letting go of the past is Forgiveness as is letting go of things that have negative connections or serve no worthwhile purpose. This makes space for positive replacements. Feng Shui recognises that clutter can make people feel disorganised, uncreative, tired, anxious and burdened. Energy or Qi is all around us, all the time, the clutter is a clutter of energies.

Positive Qi, can become blocked by clutter. When energy is blocked, it becomes stagnate and then turns to negative energy. That is why one of the main principles of Feng Shui is that you must de-clutter your home. It's important to remember that getting rid of the old makes way for the new.

Start by clearing out everything that doesn't need to be there, unload it. In order to get new things in your life you have to release old things. Look around your home. Let go of Failure. If you have relationship or collaboration problems, let go of things, letters, postcards, cards, pictures and items that are representing lack of harmony in relationships. Let go of anything representing your previous relationships that didn't work out for you. Put them all in a box and store it somewhere to tell the universe there is space for a renewed success. Let go of everything, even old images, particularly of relationships that ended. Release it all. If you do not have much time to clean and clear presently, place in closed spaces, or boxes and cover the boxes with beautiful fabrics. When clutter is visible, your sub conscious mind sends a message of chaos to the universe.

Sometimes it can be challenging to get rid of things that we don't need, but in doing so, we free up more of our energy to devote to the things we want. If you resist letting go of items because you spent money on them, then consider selling them. You can hold a garage sale, list them on Craigslist or eBay. If you still hold onto any items of ended relationships, then you are holding on to old energy patterns that block your Qi moving forward and your resistance is indicating lack and limitation, and you are not ready to move forward to your ideal relationships. Even holding onto things for a later date, or just in case is indicating lack and limitation, as well as inviting some adversity to occur.

Here's an example of relationships. When we hold on to the baggage from old relationships, they tend to carry over into new relationships, and this causes issues in the new relationship. If you were with someone for a period of time and they cheated on you, you may carry the belief that you have been burnt in this way, so you have built up resistance to complete trust and faith. This can spill over to your new partner and, even if they are not cheating, sometimes you feel there may be something they are not telling you. And it causes a fight until eventually you break up. It's the same concept with clutter in your home. If you carry all that old clutter around, there is no room in your life for new things to prosper. Abundance will pass you by because you're too busy holding on to lack and clutter.

Release an ended romantic relationship by replacing the pictures with something more general or romantic. Remove anything that constantly reminds you of the person. Return, discard, or store the items the other person left behind, including clothes, books, CDs, and DVDs. Do not keep things out of revenge or to punish someone. Release is forgiveness, not revenge or retribution. Letting go of that which does not contribute to your happiness makes room for new happiness and fulfilment.

Your living areas

Represent the present. Too much clutter creates stagnant Qi as well as inconvenience and frustration. Remove items that are from previous ailments or items given to you that you do not particularly like. Place something that makes you feel good and makes you smile. Lilac represents the frequency of releasing, use lavender oils in your soaps, lotions and cleaning products to cleanse the stagnant, dense Qi.

Outside areas

Represents the present. Clear gardens of dried plants, or rubbish lying around, clean paths and maintain this, it allows the flow of positive Qi to enter. No faded, broken items or dried plants, the positive Qi is not present in these.

The Basement or under your home/office

Represents the past. This is better place to store things, however, too much stored indicates you are trapped in the past.

The attic

Represents the future. Too much stored here can block your future and the futures of generations to come. Avoid storage above the bedrooms or lounge room.

Improve your Qi flow with FORGIVENSS and RELEASE

- Let go of possessions, emotions, and thoughts that keep you stuck, particularly of ended relationships.
- The colour violet represents forgiveness
- Elevate the level of Qi in your environment and yourself.
- Let go of photos, objects, and furnishings from your past that no longer serve you
- Reliving old memories and relationships is stagnant Qi. Let go of the past, things that have no allocated space or serve no worthwhile purpose. Remember that getting rid of the old makes

way for the new Qi. Move on to make new, happy memories. Free up the stuck, dense energy to create a brilliant future
- Have a more positive outlook and focus on the things you are grateful for. Start a gratitude journal. Each day write three things you are grateful for.
- Antiques can have mental, emotional, and even spiritual impressions attached to them, release the dense Qi of the past by using lavender, geranium, and rosemary essential oils added to water for cleaning.
- Clear and organise your home or workspace to get the energy flowing, and prepare for new people, experiences, and opportunities into your life. Create space for good fortune to enter your life by creating an uncluttered space in every room.

.

Activate your relationships and collaboration

A Feng Shui consultant uses the combination of Space Feng Shui and Time Feng Shui.

Space Feng Shui assessments determine the directions Qi flows in and around your physical environment. This includes General space orientation and activation of the home or office as well as activating and enhancing Personal Space Feng Shui based on an individual's Personal fortune directions to improve/increase Success, Health, Relationships and Growth. Time Feng Shui is the analysis of time cycles or Visiting Energy Assessments and the nature of specific energy flows of time cycles. All have their appointed compass direction, each of these nine directions have significant purposes, and the southwest corner of your home or workplace is your general relationships sector along with other compass directions for collaboration, as well as relationship with self.

Personal fortune directions or Personal Space Feng Shui as mentioned above can only be assessed on an individual basis where a person's birthdate and other factors are required for accurate assessment. General Space Feng Shui is universal, the following pages contain general space relationships, collaboration and relationship to self-practice.

Feng Shui and quantum physics teaches that everything in our physical environment carries an energy that is moving our lives forward in that direction. By placing in our physical surroundings objects or images that have a positive personal meaning, we are activating and sending the Qi in this direction every time we look at it. Even if we think we do not see it any longer, it is still registering the message on a sub-conscious level.

Personal Intimate Relationship
If you want the ideal partner, love, romance or marriage luck, a better relationship with your significant other, a better sex life, a deeper connection, enhance your relationship, more time together -- it all can be yours! You can enhance or improve every aspect of your love life for romantic dreams to come true. Activate in the bedroom and living room only.

For a single person part of attracting a partner is being open to receiving the love and romance coming your way. This requires you to forgive and release the past as in the previous chapter, it also requires you to build a romantic nest that supports a coupled relationship.

Ensure your bedroom is comfortable for two people. If one side of your bed is placed against a wall or is hiding behind the door with a single bedside table you may have a difficulty finding a love relationship. For a balanced, harmonious relationship ensure your bed has balanced energy on both sides to accommodate a couple. For a lasting intimate relationship both partners must feel equal and respected. Provide two bedside tables and include a lamp even if you're sleeping alone, set up a nightstand on both sides of your bed, to accommodate the needs of your future partner.

Available space invites free flowing Qi. Ensure you have free space in your wardrobe, without free flow of energy more opportunities are not invited.

Your bedroom, bathroom and kitchen are your home trinity, ensure it is clean and uncluttered with no expired products. This will sooner or later reflect in the energy of your love relationship if it one or more are left unattended.

Clearly visualise your life with the man or the woman of your dreams. Write this in a journal. Write in the now as though you are watching a movie about it. The stronger and clearer you are in stating what you would like, the easier it is for the universe to send you your heart's desire. Write a list of all the qualities your ideal partner has. Are they smart, caring, a world traveller, or a homebody who loves to spend quiet evenings watching movies with you on the couch? What are they like to you? How would that look, feel, taste, smell? Bring that sense into your home with specific images, colours, and scents that reflect the energy you want. Do not place sad, or broken heart images. Place images and items in pairs to send the message of positive relationships such as two rose quartz crystals or images that present two loving people, birds, romance or marriages.

For a woman looking for love and romance, place a vase filled with peonies flowers or an image of this. This is not for a coupled or married woman because it will bring in intimate male relationships from outside your marriage.

If you are married or have a significant other it is essential that harmony, balance, respect and a romantic nest is created in the bedroom that supports the relationship.

Position Bed Harmoniously. Position the bed so that both your crowns face a solid wall, allowing full view of the room and its entry while lying in bed. Avoid placing the bed in line with a doorway, since this can cause feelings of vulnerability and defensiveness. Also avoid alignment with the bathroom door, as this can contribute to feeling drained, tired or having restless sleep patterns which can lead to friction in a relationship.

If you are satisfied with your relationships and would like a positive energetic boost, add a candle to the Southwest. Or an image or statue of a divine mother like Kuan Yin, Mother Mary, Bhagavathi or Isis for tenderness. Ensure your wedding picture or personal pictures with your romantic partner are on display.

Ensure you have a solid headboard this represents support, and energetically brings both sides of the bed together, creating harmonious union for partners. If possible, avoid metal bedframes they enhance the water element and water should never be in the bedroom. Metal is yang Qi and attracts unsettling dreams.

Too much stuff piled in a bedroom (or any room for that matter) is a huge energetic distraction that subconsciously pulls us away from our focus and each other. The bedroom should be a space designed for rest, rejuvenation, romance, and relief from the outside world. Remove the clutter such as computers, exercise equipment, paperwork, kids' projects, or piled clothes, find a place for them. Just be careful not to clutter up another part of your home, everything must have its place or it is considered as clutter.

Display Romantic Artwork in your home, surround yourselves with art that displays love and romance for two. Do not place images that has a single man or single woman in it, or one that has three or more people in it. This brings a third party into your bedroom.

Hang a six tube metal wind chime or a crystal in the center of the bedroom to enhance the energy in the space. Ensure the wind chime has a gentle, pleasant sound for both of you.

For a coupled or married woman place an image or statue of a divine mother such as Mother Mary, Kuan Yin or Isis to invite compassion.

Combinations of red and gold or purple and silver attract more passion and romance into your life, use these colours for you bedding or throw pillows, you can wear them too.

Relationship can be aggravated by health or money issues, domineering children or in-laws. If you have children or in-laws sleeping southwest of the home, this invites them to be controlling or interfere in your intimate relationships. Hang an image or place a symbolic item of the two of you in your lounge room to reclaim control over your relationship.

If you are in business with your romantic partner also activate the Southwest in your workplace. Disply personal pictures of you with your romantic partner.

At the reception of a wedding place romantic pictures of the married couple to invite more love and happiness. This can be in gold frames or in poster form.

Family Relationships

To have a family that is loving and supportive at all times is a blessing. To have a healthy, beautiful and happy environment to share with your family is to be blessed twice.

The art and science of Feng Shui is intricate and complex. Houses and their surroundings are studied carefully for their influence on people living in the house. The quality of energy in your home determines the quality of your everyday family interactions and when Feng Shui principles are implemented, this creates positive energy flow in the environment for all family members, both young and old. Feng Shui practices invite better relationships with your children or your family and will help you bring more peace and understanding into your family life.

Areas of your home represents a specific area of your life:

The Centre

The center of your home is considered very important, because it is from the center that all other areas of your home draw their energy nourishment. The center is called the heart of the home, or the yin yang point. The more open and happy the center of the home is, the happier and more open the people who live in that home tend to be. Take good care of your center by creating vibrant and harmonious energy there, place happy items and images, what happiness means to you and your family.

Lounge/Family Room

The energy of family harmony is closely connected to the family bagua area of your home. Place in this area elements of vibrant wood, a fountain for positive Qi flow, clear or rose quartz crystals as well as happy family photos.

Express Happiness

Quantum physics states like attracts like energy. A home that is clean, clutter free and loved will attract and promote harmonious communication between all family members. Organise your home so that everything has its place. Most importantly, express love and care with all your home contents, this indicates good support, care, happiness and well-being of your family. Create a home that is beautiful, joyful and full of love.

Family Collaboration

For better collaboration between family members and friends, place a picture of the entire family, or members of the family with whom you would like to collaborate in the East direction of your lounge/family room, which is the general direction for family. The East is connected with a forest that represents a family of trees and wildlife, place a family tree here. If you work with family, activate collaboration in the East direction of your workplace as well. Avoid placing wastebaskets or clutter here. The lounge/family room is considered the area where the family comes together. How the space is organised can help the whole family live together in harmony.

Relationships with Children and Grandchildren

The west is the area of purity. Enhance this direction in your lounge/family room with items or pictures related to children such as Images of children or children playing, or family pictures of you with your children. You can also place an item or image of a laughing Buddha to increase happiness. If work with children, also activate the West direction in your workplace with pictures of the children you work with or care for.

Feng Shui principles in children's rooms creates a healthy, loving and safe environment. A child's room created with Feng Shui applications will serve as an emotional and physical support during the experiences of your child's growth as well as harmonise their relationships. How healthy and fresh is the air your child breathes in? How much natural light does your child get? What is the quality of artificial lights in your child's room? Considering the presence of all electrical appliances, what is the level of EMF radiation your child is exposed to? What is the level of clutter in the room?

A good energy foundation in your children's rooms is very important. Ensure your child's bedroom is a clean, clutter free space for positive energy to flow easily. Also allow fresh air to enter and position the bedhead to a solid wall. When you have a solid energy foundation in your child's room, be sure you allow for maximum expression of his or her energy. Let your child choose art for his or her space, also display their art around your home. The more control your child has over his or her space, the more empowered and happy they will feel.

Motherhood and Compassion

Southwest stands for motherhood and compassion. Create a gentle ease of love and support in the way you relate to yourself and others. *"Be gentle first with yourself if you wish to be gentle with others."* ~Lama Yeshe.

When we feel compassion for others, we feel kindness toward them, empathy, and a desire to help. It's the same when you are compassionate toward yourself. Self-compassion creates a caring space within you that is free of judgment. An important part of living a happy and fulfilling life includes being part of sharing, helping and supporting people you care about. It also includes being kind to strangers, and learning to replace envy and anger with understanding and empathy. Allow yourself to see that *everything* around you is sacred.

Enhance compassion in this direction of your lounge room or bedroom by placing an image or statue of your 'Mother of

Compassion': Kuan Yin, Mother Mary, Tara, Mother Theresa, Isis or someone who represents compassion to you.
-Feel more compassion for yourself, others, and for the world you live in
- Go easy on yourself when you try new things or make mistakes
- Show trust in others and treat them with patience and gentleness
- Have patience to listen to your inner voice and the advice of others. Be more open to others

Empowerment/Self-Empowerment
Manifest Your Power by being open to transform your life. When you start to change things, make the changes with the right attitude. Proceed fearlessly. Do not complain about the changes you need to make or it will block the ease of making them. Look for support available to you and believe you will have all the help you need. Let go of things and situations with joy. When something does not serve you anymore, be thankful for what you received from it. Recycle it to bless someone else. Place ornaments and move furniture with a sense of blessing. In between every change, take time to experience the impact and enjoy the process.

--Forgive yourself and release the past. Write a list of what you forgive yourself for or say it out aloud.

-Have courage to make necessary changes

-Create collaboration with all of the support available to you

-Love yourself and release judgment. Hold the intention that it will empower you to do your Feng Shui decluttering, cleaning, and activations.

- Be more outgoing

- Learn how and when to say no. This is a crucial step towards reclaiming your personal sense of empowerment. You control your own choices.

General Supportive Luck

Have more friends, enhance your general supportive luck and friendships, mentoring relationships, your relationship with your father, and relationships with your children by placing Items or images in the northwest of your Home, Office or Yard, such as Images of supportive kinds of relationships: fatherhood, personal pictures with your father, mentors, friendships, or an image of helping hands. Do not place Fire elements. No wastebaskets, clutter, or yard waste in these corners because the accumulation creates density and slows the flow of positive Qi.

When you work in business with your friends, father, or children, enhance the Northwest area in your workplace as well.

The TRINITY of LUCK

In Feng Shui, there are three categories which describe the type of luck we experience in our lives, they are:

Heaven Luck- This refers to the karma, destiny, health types, astrological horoscope and the family environment you were born into and is determined by the cycles of time. This type of luck cannot be controlled. You can however, through astrological cycles or the Chinese Astrology Almanac, also known as the Tung Shu prepare for times when you are more likely to experience positive and negative points towards key areas in your life such as health, relationships, career, or finances. It helps to take note of astrological periods. This indicates where your key life lessons will be more likely to occur. Your astrological chart also helps determine areas where you are more likely to experience luck potential. These astrological events can affect communications, contractual problems, delays, travel, machinery breakdown and times of change and unexpected news. To make the most of your overall luck potential, you should develop a positive, progressive attitude while applying Feng Shui principles to your home and work environment, as well as keeping up to date with major astrological changes in your life. Luck is ultimately when skill and knowledge, plus the right attitude, meet opportunity. Feng Shui can help the flow of Qi that attracts positive energy, this increases your abundance opportunities.

Earth Luck - This type of luck is determined by our surroundings for example our home or workspace and the way in which we direct ourselves with positive or negative energy combinations, within and around the earth. This type of luck can be improved and enhanced when Feng Shui is correctly applied to your home or work environment. It deals with balance, element cycles, mathematical probability factors, magnetic orientation, surrounding landform and time dimensional analysis.

Human Luck - This refers to your personal attitude, education, managerial and financial ability, lifestyle, virtues, the choices that you make and your personal quest for knowledge. As an individual, you have full control over this type of luck, and when it is combined with Earth Luck through the correct application of Feng Shui, you increase your experience for greater harmony, contentment and success. To truly experience the joys which life can offer, you must first examine your attitude and sense of self. Change your attitude and you can quite literally change your life. You can utilise positive symbols, words and images within your surroundings to help focus and connect your personal aspirations with the appropriate Earth Luck location combinations.

- Learn to recognise your negative self talk. We all do it to some extent. Change it to an uplifting phrase.

- The positive and negative behaviours in your life have had many years to shape you into the unique individual that you have now become. Learn to look at yourself objectively in order to recognise certain conditioned responses and patterned behaviour, this can be enlightening.

- Acknowledge each positive step that you take forward.

- Surround yourself with positive friends and family who will encourage and support you.

- Actively seek to learn and experience as much as you can from the people and environment around you. Learn from someone who has what you want. Knowledge is life with wings. Find yourself a mentor someone who you aspire to be like and admire for what they have achieved in their life. Observe the ways in which they conduct themselves.

- If you find yourself feeling negative resolve it through forgiveness. You may not alter a situation immediately, but you can take full control of your response to the situation and how you ultimately deal with it.

General Collaboration

Improving collaboration amplifies your efforts. Remove any symbols that contradict collaboration such as: images of yourself alone; images of animals attacking, battles, or other tragedies, images of people or animals facing away from each other. Activating relationship directions of your workplace improves your professional collaboration and activating the relationship direction in your lounge room or bedroom will improve your spiritual collaboration. To increase collaboration, place the pictures or items for your activations together so they give a feeling of togetherness. Put these pictures in a fuchsia frame.

-Learn from others, there are gems in all we experience

- Share the workload. This will invite a positive flow of Qi for all.

- Share a common sense of accomplishment. Be happy for another's success, when you rejoice for another your rewards increase.

Enhance Your Connection to Heaven

Activate your Home or Office For in Relationships and Collaboration

The direction connected to the Northwest is called Helpful People and Blessings or Connection to Heaven and help from Heaven, it also relates to patriarch and patronage luck representing the full force of Yang energy. This direction within the home or workspace aligns your connection with the outside world including your mentors, work colleagues, friends, networking, benefactors and business prospects.

Place an activation here for the energy to help attract beneficial people in your life. We all need somebody to help us. We all need a mentor. Mentors do not only refer to people who are in power who can teach us things or help us in achieving our goals, this also refers to people who may not be our senior in stature, age, experience, but are around us can is able to contribute to our success. Place silver bells and a singing bowl in this direction. Avoid water images as they will deplete the favourable energy.

In Feng Shui, by activating our Mentor's Luck we start to attract people who help us along the way. Begin by being positive yourself this starts the flow of a powerful positive aura, which in turn will attract people who are also positive.

This direction also supports the energy of travel, if you would like to travel more, express this energy here. Travel is also beneficial to health, new environments equals a new flow of Qi. Place travel photos, and maps. Photos of people who have helped you grow in life are also good to display or spiritual mentors, symbols, teachers, and angels that support us. Do not put a fire element, candles in the Northwest of home, lounge room, or other important rooms because it symbolizes fire at heaven's gate. If you have a fireplace in the Northwest, place a bowl of still water next to it, the water element represents diminishing the fire energy.

Business Collaboration

Enhance relationships with your business or work colleagues.

For better collaboration with your manager, supervisor, mentor, personal coach, or boss, activate the northwest direction in your workplace, it stands for hierarchy and is connected with heaven, the father, the stars, and the planets. Place a picture of you and your intended collaborator along with their business card attached to yours. If you want help from powerful and influential people, this is the sector to activate. Display a wealth ship (with sails, no cannon holes) here and pile up with coins, jewellery or gemstones.

For better collaboration with your work colleagues or business partners, activate the Southwest direction in your workplace. This direction represents general collaboration. Place a team picture or a ceramic circle of animals or people.

If you are in business with your romantic partner, mother, or children, also activate the Southwest in your workplace with personal pictures on display.

When working with others in your office, add a round table, this shape enhances collaboration and a mastermind of problem solving ideas.

Arrange the surface of your desk with Feng Shui principles. The nine directions or bagua is a map that can be applied to your desktop as well as your computer, just as it would be applied to the floor plan of a home or office. Different areas of the bagua are associated with different areas of your life, for relationships place as follows:
-The center front of the desk should be free of clutter and represents your career. The dominant colour here should be black, also add a motivational quotes here.
-The center back of your desk has to do with fame and your reputation. Place a red item or colour here, a nameplate, your

business cards, or an image of yourself accomplishing something great.

-The front right corner represents helpers and travel. Place a grey item or colour here including your address book, a travel guide or an image of a holiday location.

-The left center of your desk place a family photo, in a wooden frame with something green on it. This is the area associated with family relationships.

-The back right corner of the desk is associated with intimate relationships. Place a photo of your significant other, or add a flower to attract romance.

-    For the computer place icons such as your email, internet browser, or photo folders in the southwest of the screen which is the top right hand corner of the computer screen to enhance your general relationship flow. For Personal fortune relationships, this can be established through a Personal Feng Shui analysis by a Feng Shui consultant.

For those who have a home office or work from home, you can apply the same Feng Shui principles as in any other work environment. Keep the entrance of your home neat, clean, and free of clutter, including the entrance to your office space. Even if clients do not attend this workplace this is essential in opening the flow of energy and welcoming positive improvements to your work life.

Education Collaboration
For a student who would like to have a great collaboration with their teacher activate collaborative help with your studies or work. Place books, study material or work related papers in the northeast direction.

The type of teacher desire to collaborate with will determine which area you will activate. Activate your workplace or study area for a teacher of knowledge and skills, such as your business mentor or personal coach. For a teacher of spiritual wisdom, activate your living room and bedroom by placing an image of you with your teacher, a book or material done by your teacher.

Your Personal Fortune Directions and Time Feng Shui for Money and Success
Your Personal Fortune directions are based on your Kua number, and has a greater effect for you personally than general space Feng Shui. The areas include success, relationships, health and growth, and is established by gender, as well as date of birth. Money is associated with success, when you know your Personal Fortune Directions you can face it for added success, as well as place activations in these

directions to amplify your personal success. There are four misfortune directions as well. When you are aware of these directions you can cure and ensure specific placements are not hindering your success. To establish the fortune colour, element, shape, fabric and other aspects for your relationships and collaboration requires a Personal Fortune direction analysis, a Feng Shui Consultant is recommended.

Never place anything into your space that you do not love just because you are told you to do so. Feng Shui is about creating a positive flow of Qi as well as creating a living space that feeds your soul and uplifts your spirits. Objects you don't love will have the opposite effect. The more personal the objects are to you, the more Qi they will generate. Representations of items do not require to be only one thing such as Eastern symbols. An example is the Chinese symbolism for a tortoise, the Celestial Guardian of the North, this can be represented by any tortoise, live, image or object.

Relationship and collaboration enhancers

Feng Shui cures obstacles, strengthens intentions and addresses how the Qi flows through an environment. A value of Feng Shui is to bring our awareness to those areas of our life which are not in harmony with our intention. There are several approaches to making these adjustments and enhancements by adjusting the home or workplace environment, even ourselves. We can remove negative Qi and other dense factors that distract, slow down or, in some other way, divert our intention for desired relationships.

The Bagua directions of a home or workplace divides the structure or individual spaces into nine areas of life activity and these are connected by distinct energy fields of the spaces along with objects, images, plants animals and people. Through people and animals emotions and personal practises are also emitted. When you improve the energy of your home, you change yourself and your life and by applying the Feng Shui principles for self enhancement you evolve to fulfil your desires. Author *Napoleon Hill* explains, *"Our brains become magnetised with the dominating thoughts which we hold in our minds, and, by means with which no man is familiar, these 'magnets' attract to us the forces, the people, the circumstances of life which harmonise with the nature of our dominating thoughts."*

CLARITY

Clarity is the quality of being easily understood, expressed, remembered and of being easily seen or heard

Feng Shui principles assist you in communicating more clearly in your relationships by expressing your needs and desires openly, earnestly and wholly. Through establishing and applying your desires in your environment it creates impressive results from your efforts and avoids misunderstandings.

Clarity begins with deciding what you want. What kind of a relationship. How do you see a harmonious collaboration? Prioritise areas where you require fast results. Determine exactly what you want to accomplish. Bring a clear, accurate message of your desired outcome for your relationships and collaboration. Place symbol, images or objects reflecting the outcome that you want to create. Let go of images that no longer clearly represent your intentions. Take care of what has not been completed now, just by starting and ticking off even your simplest tasks invites the positive Qi of clarity.

To send the best message about abundance and invite clarity, clean water features. Light up your home, workplace, yard and entry. Add bright objects and plants. Place happy items an images in the eight directions including the Centre of your home or workspace that represent romance, family and Children.

Ensure the entrance and exterior to your home or workplace is well lit and has clear messages showing the world to recognise and respond to your personality or business, as well as indicating that a very successful person is inside. Also place happy items or images outside. Do not hang dark or depressing images.

CELEBRATION
South stands for fame and recognition as well as music, celebration, and festivity, activate the South area by placing orange objects in living room or workplace. Unless you want to get pregnant do not activate celebration in the bedroom.

Celebrate your efforts and accomplishments, changes, significant dates and celebrate yourself! Cooked a great meal, celebrate, completed your tasks, celebrate. Add the positive flow of celebration to anything you choose to rejoice for.

Manifest more joy showing off your awards and place them in gold frames to invite abundance. This will give you more to celebrate.

Celebrate your accomplishments by throwing a party. Do not wait for others. Create celebrations for yourself. Feng Shui is a consistent celebration of positive flowing Qi. Include children in your parties, because they represent the fortune of the family.

If you want to have a baby make space for your baby by clearing the clutter under the bed. Elephants are considered a wish-granting animal. Place a pair of wooden elephants on both sides of your bedroom door as if they were walking into the room, so they make your wish walk through that same door. Also place an image of children or a stuffed animal in the west direction of your bedroom to invite energies supportive of conception and birth.

To heal a broken heart use orange essential oils. This is considered as a natural antidepressant and an effective treatment for emotional downs. The oil is used to bring peace and calm to an emotional situation while inviting serenity and harmony. Add orange essential oil to a spray bottle filled with water, and spray around your spaces each day. Ancient wisdom praises the use of oranges to help peel away your problems. Place the peels from the oranges, plus two cups of Epsom salts, into a bath and soak in it. Your enthusiasm and optimism will return.

HONESTY and HONOUR

Honour is connected to the east and power of the dragon, a symbol of power, truth, and magic. Place Dragon Symbol or object in your workspace or lounge room lower than eye level so it does not overpower you and enjoy the Dragon's precious cosmic breath.

Improve Human Luck: Feng Shui helps create an environment to change old habits, create more self-discipline and double your talents to their full potential. HONOUR is important, Eastern cultures practice Honour.

When the flow of life is good, ride the wave. When the flow of life is not great, check to see if it is keeping you from doing what you want to do. Contemplate your behaviour. Are your actions, thoughts and feelings honourable? If not what mental programs can you change and emotions can you release.

Keep structure and good life management, practice self-help/development. These are a strong indicators of how we can change our programs. Discipline yourself to fulfil your destiny and to fully express who you are. Make it easier to stick to your intentions and actions with your family and clients. Surround yourself with people who are truthful. Be more honest with yourself and others.

Improve Heavenly Luck: Practise spiritual lessons, Qigong, yoga, prayer, meditation and positive affirmations.

Improve Earth Luck: Your environment, home and workplace, is a greater body surrounding your physical body. Every object in your home or workplace is like a cell in the greater body. And as part of the unified field of the whole, will affect your body and physical experience. There are unseen links of energy between every material thing. All part of the Quantum Physics field. This can be improved with Feng Shui practices by allowing the positive flow of Qi.

For your workspace display a pair of Fu Dogs at the entrance door to protect you against office politics and corporate power struggles.

PURITY

There are 5 levels of purity: Physical Home, office and body, Etheric, Emotional, Mental and Spiritual

Activate your Home or Office For in Relationships and Collaboration

Creating purity is essential if your thoughts and feelings are cluttered or chaotic, you are addicted to something or you feel abused or that people violate your boundaries.

Meditations, or exercises such as Qigong and yoga assist in creating stillness within the active mind. Visualise the light of the sun in your body and home with a light meditation. Open the windows and doors to bring in light and activate your senses. When natural light is low, use lamps in the dark areas. Ensure the four corners of each room in your home or workspace are well-lit. If you are unable to light all four corners of each space, ensure that every corner of your lounge room has light.

Clean your home or workspace with lavender oils mixed in with your cleaning products. Wash your physical body every day. Use lavender soaps or add lavender oil to your shower gel, lavender helps release toxins and old energies from your aura.

To invite purity into your body and new possibilities into your life, create space for what you want. Even the best activations are impeded upon in a cluttered or dirty environment, ensure you dust your furniture too.

Do not display broken objects. The life force or Qi in these objects are broken and gluing does not restore the Qi.

JOY

The West is the direction for Joy it also represents communication, and children's luck.

If you would like to appreciate everything your senses experience or you lack joy, feel sad or are depressed. Place fun, humorous items here. Add fabrics, colourful artwork, bright pillows or objects bright colours to lead eyes from colour to colour. Peach and orange are the best for joy, red and warm yellows add joy too. Activate in the lounge room for everyone to invite more joyful communication. Place joyful images, toys and smiling people. Allow more sunlight to enter the spaces and open windows to let the wind bring new Qi into the home. If you cannot open your windows, use air fresheners and burn candles. White and black colours do not create joy. Exposed beams in your entrance or lounge room can create sadness for everyone in the family, cover them in fabric or paint them the same colour as the ceiling.

TRANSPARENCY

Invite clearness of mind, body, emotions and environment. Ensure that your lounge room and workspace are clean and uncluttered. Become more organised and get your business or personal records in order.

Etheric transparency

The etheric field is the energy body known as the first layer in the human energy field or commonly known as the aura. This field has less dense Qi than the Qi that surrounds the physical body. This energetic body or aura is fed by the air we breathe and the impact of our surroundings. Our etheric field is influenced by the level of Qi in a room. Low energy levels of Qi create negative thoughts and depressed feelings where high energy levels of Qi help us feel raised and happy. Ensure you maintain high levels of Qi by opening windows and doors. An oil burner, incense, ioniser or air purifier will enhance the positive flow. Ensure the air you breathe is clean. Be mindful of the images, objects, and paintings you display, this can create a negative impression on you.

Emotional transparency

Emotional fields from you and your family or past inhabitants may linger in your home or workplace. There may have been a break up or constant fighting. Place a little salt and rice in all of the corners of your spaces as a gesture of abundance and gratitude and remove it after one day. Also place water with sea salt in the centre of the home or workspace for seven days.

If you are experiencing arguments this may be associated with your kitchen. If your stove is opposite a sink this indicates disharmony, fire fights with water, water boils. Hang a pakua crystal between the stove and sink to unify fire and water. These are special 8-sided mirrors used to cure negative Qi. Door handles can also be associated with arguments if they hit against each other. Tie a red ribbon to the handles to symbolically establish unity between these arguing door handles then cut the ribbon evenly and tie them onto the handles.

Mental transparency:

Occasional sanctuary is required in our lives, particularly when you want to put ideas into action, slow down, restore clarity or when you want to be more relaxed mentally. For mental transparency create a room with less furniture, fewer books, fewer ornaments, and fewer things to tend. It can also be a chair and window focused on a view that is spacious or a bathtub filled with essential oils and natural suds. These are vital spaces to recharge our own energetic batteries, after all we are beings that contain electricity.

Also clean your desk when you finish working to be ready for fresh ideas. Keep alarm clocks at least five feet from your head when sleeping the electrical field disturbs your sleep and interfere with your focus.

FAITH

Have strong belief and trust in yourself as well as with the ancient art of Feng Shui. Create the new energy you need to manifest your intentions. Change the way you think, feel, and act. Apply the principles and invite your chosen positive destiny to unfold. Have patience with yourself and others. Recognise the results from your Feng Shui practices. Positive and negative responses can occur as you begin making changes. Respond in a positive way, and feel relief that there is finally a logical explanation for misfortunes in your life. Feng Shui changes can stir up energy and temporarily upset order, but it will calm down as the energy finds a new order. If you resist you lose focus and concentration. Resistance leads to fear and anger, have faith in your choices.

TRANSFORMATION

Have you ever thought, if only! Or if I could turn back time. Forgive and release the past, say goodbye to old behaviours and beliefs that no longer serve you, and say hello to a more positive incarnation of yourself, there always has and always will be time, life offers to many wonderful opportunities, you just have to invite them in and lay the groundwork for a better tomorrow to welcome your new success for what you truly desire.

Boost your romance, live a more conscious lifestyle, get the support you need to pursue your dreams. Change the way you feel in your surroundings, change your thought patterns or how you feel about yourself and recognise your transformations.

By applying these Feng Shui practices you have placed yourself in a transformation whirlwind, a waterfall of change. Some people feel overwhelmed and disoriented, which indicates that something is changing. Things must change to allow for the new to come. *Einstein's definition of insanity, "Insanity is doing the same thing over and over again and expecting different results."*. You are sane! Stay with it and look for the positive changes from your new energy flow!

Ask yourself, do I feel:
Happy and more confident that everything will be all right. Peaceful in my own home. Excited about my life and the changes I want to create. Comfortable in my space and no longer running away from it. A need to change many things in my life. A sense of accomplishment because I have made more changes

Activate your Home or Office For in Relationships and Collaboration

in one week than I have in years. Able to handle things and climb out of a depression. Open to others and myself.

How has my thinking changed? Do I feel less fear, doubt, limitation, or loneliness? Do I express more power, self-esteem, and success?

Notice the changes in your relationships or collaboration. Passion and romance may have entered your life, an ideal significant other, harmony with your children or better circumstances in your workplace.

Notice other changes such as your activity level. You might complete little jobs around the house, spend more time playing with your children or associating with friends, take up painting or writing, or express your feelings better. People around you may be offering more encouragement to pursue your dreams, help you find the right resources, or help you find the ideal partner.

Start a positive flow journal. Observe and record positive changes in your life. Write gratitude statements. Write in your journal daily, use blue ink, this is the colour for power. Recording your positive flow will enhance a chain of positive change in your own experiences and empower others to become active in their own good fortune and luck.

TENDERNESS

Transform your bedroom into a place of nurturing sensuality and healing beauty, a place that has balanced energy for two people, not just one. Be sure you genuinely love the way your bedroom looks and feels from wall colour and window treatment to your bed linens and bedroom art.

Create tenderness for yourself and your loved ones, find it easier to express appreciation and tenderness to your loved ones and be more open to receive tender attention from others. This is the most feminine or yin of all the bagua directions and is governed by the element Earth bringing essence of care, warmth, love and relationship. Place symbols of tenderness.

In your lounge room place a six-rod hollow metal wind chime. Wind chimes attract good chi. Ensure that it is a six-rod hollow metal wind chime. The wind chime is the best moving metal activator because it removes the density of the earth by attracting the energy of the earth in its hollow tubes. Change any angles or sharp edges of furniture, columns, shelves, pointed plants, ornaments, or objects to point away from where you and your loved ones sit. Hang crystals at large windows to reflect sunlight and create rainbows.

In your child's bedroom hang images of dragonflies or butterflies. Do not place tigers or lions, they represent predators nor negative messages such as 'Keep Out', this will influence your tender relationship with your child as well as harmony in the whole home.

Feng Shui practice also means creating tenderness in the gifts you give your loved ones. Give personalised gifts with your heart. Place your gift in soft tissue paper. Do not give clocks or watches these symbolise that you do not have time for them or that time is running out.

General and quick tips

There can be many subtle factors in an environment that supports us with either positive or negative results in our relationships. Awareness and observation can move you from the negative to the positive flow.

Dining Room

Hang a mirror with a gold frame reflecting the dining table. This doubles abundance and the amount of people sharing a meal. Keep fresh fruit or flowers on the table. This brings life, energy, and invites good health and is doubled by the mirror.

Bedroom

The bedroom is for rest, rejuvenation and romance. Ensure your bed and bedroom support this.

Position the bed where the headboard is against a solid wall and that you can clearly see the entry door. Do not sleep under a window. Moonlight on the head, brings lack of focus during the daytime. Ensure your bed has balanced energy on both sides for example do not have one side of the bed up against a wall. Ensure both sides of the bed have a side table, light and a pleasant view. Position other furniture harmoniously. Good furniture arrangements play a significant role in Feng Shui. It is important have a clear path to enter your bedroom, no matter what section of the house it's located in. Try to make sure that large furniture is not placed too near the doorway.

Avoid storing a lot of electronics in bedrooms. The constant hum of electricity and blinking lights disrupts the flow of energy, and it is difficult to relax in that environment. If you must have electronics in the room, be sure to put them away when you're not using them. Place alarm clocks at least 5 or 6 feet away from body unless they run on batteries.

Ensure you do not have a mirror reflecting the bed. A mirror that reflects your image when you are in bed scatters thoughts and create negative dreams. It also complicates a marriage through a third person or creates loneliness. If you are single and you want to attract the right intimate relationship this indicates you already have somebody. If you already have a significant other this invites interferences in your relationship. It's best to avoid putting a television in the room, this affects the energy in the room, and it also reflects the bed. If you choose to have this place a cover over it when not in use, this also preserves tenderness.

Avoid family pictures in your bedroom, this is your private space and a place for you and your significant other. Family images here impede on your experience to fully enjoy your partner. If you have religious images or items, place them so that they are not directed at your bed.

Ensure items in the room have a proper place, and group them in twos, for example two candles, one each on the bedside tables. Hang pictures in pairs and keep your throw pillows balanced on your bed. Even if you are single, do not just have one towel hanging in the bathroom. Ensure everything is in pairs. There must also be order and unity to the room. Visual symmetry provides peace of mind, and it keeps the energy flowing through the room evenly.

Do not put water in the room, actual water or images with water, this attracts more unsettling dreams. No live plants or flowers because they have too much active yang energy for the bedroom, calm yin energy is required.

Avoid work related items or exercise equipment. The bedroom is a passive space, not yang energy. Place your work desk or computer elsewhere. If you have no other place for a home office ensure the computer and all the work related items are put away before going to bed so you do not see it from your bed. The also applies to exercise equipment, place it elsewhere, not under the bed otherwise the active energy will promote a restless sleep.

Exposed beams over a bed symbolises division and invites separation. When sleeping under a beam people have problems because these structures put pressure on their aura. Beams straight across over the head symbolises the guillotine and good energy will be cut off before it benefits you. Thin and sharp beams have greater impact than beams that are flat and wide. Diagonal beams indicate that the good energy will start to flow but will not finish right. Sitting under beams with another for several hours has the same effect as sleeping under beams. Move your bed if is under a beam. If your space is limited and your bed cannot be moved, cover the beam with fabric or paint the beam to match the ceiling to symbolise unification. No see through fabric.

Sleeping in a room where the street traffic faces you directly is a negative Feng Shui situation. The lights of the cars represent the eyes of the tiger stalking and attacking you. Place window coverings such as heavy curtains to block out the lights and hang a pakua mirror on the outside of the window.

Bathroom
Ensure that your bathroom is clean and organised and has a sense of beauty and pampering energy. Do not place photographs of friends or family members, as well as awards.

These are drain areas, this tells the Universe you are flushing it all away.

To create tenderness in your bathroom ensure there is a pleasant smell, soft soap and bath linens, a closed toilet lid and bathroom door.

Front Door
Let go of failure. Remove anything representing your previous relationships that didn't work out for you. Look at the images hanging on the walls in your home, especially in your entrance, living room, bedroom and your workspace. Are they reminding you of a relationship that is over? It's important that you do not place items or images of something that has ended at your entrance. Your entrance is the first impression of success when you or someone comes in to your home or workspace. Hang something more inspiring.

Start with your entry point also known as the mouth of Qi, and this includes your front door. It is the energy connection of your home. It is where the Qi enters along with what you and others bring or take with you. When you leave, you take what you're feeling with you into your day. When you come home, you bring in all that has happened to you throughout the day. The first priority for your mouth of Qi is to clear the clutter from around your door. If you and your family store shoes, coats, equipment, toys, or any other items by the front door, move them. The clutter blocks the free flow of energy, and it prevents success from entering your life.

Cleansing

Energy can neither be created nor destroyed; rather, it transforms from one form to another. When unpleasant feelings linger, space cleansing the environment transforms the energy to positive Qi leaving it lighter, healthier and happier, this creates more success. Everything that happens in an environment including conflict, trauma, and illness leave imprints and can attract other unwanted dense energy unless they are intentionally cleared. Subtle traces of past events can make places feel happy or sad. Replacing old carpet or furnishings, clutter management and redecorating all help to transform the negative dense Qi as well as cleaning the environment with lavender oils. Place a few drops of lavender oil in your cleaning products.

General

Add indoor plants and trees whenever you want growth. Avoid the cactus, as spikes invite criticism when grown inside. Try placing them in places where you spend or would like to spend positive time. The Qi or life-force of the plant, will energise the space as well as naturally remove indoor toxins and purify the air we breathe. Just remember that dead plants are a source of negative energy. If the plant is not blossoming, do not leave it sitting in your room to stagnate the flow you're trying to create.

Add some motion to a space that is stuck. A stuck space usually reflects a stuck life. Move things around the room this helps liven the atmosphere. The Feng shui number to help guide you through this process of getting unstuck is twenty-seven. Just by moving twenty-seven things around a space whether it's a paper clip or a desk can bring positive energy to a room that was previously lacking it.

Welcoming, uplifting art should be hung in gathering spaces like a lounge room. Avoid solitary images in art, in and out of the bedroom. Pictures of one person indicate the idea of being alone. This is not supportive when you are seeking a relationship or you are currently in one that you are building upon. Also avoid images such as storms, dead flowers and an uninhabited winter landscape. If you have an air conditioning unit in the southwest of your bedroom or lounge room warm it up with a red mat, an image of fire burning, or of a romantic couple.

Connect to your space personally to empower your life. Display your trophies, favourite art or patterns you love will to help forge a strong bond between you and your environment.

In order to make a room look and feel magnificent, you must think about adding gravity and balance to the space. Think about your home or workspace as a living, breathing entity that wants to feel the same. A bare dining or coffee table with art on the walls feels very different to a table that has a centrepiece displayed. This centrepiece creates visual focus that organises the room in a new way, helping it to appear more settled.

Open space welcomes new opportunities and open space gives relationships room to flourish and thrive. Clear space for happy conversations. By removing non-essential excess, it allows the flow for comfort and nestled joy.

Along with structure, items and colours your words create your environment. Something as subtle and innocent as a word enters our subconscious and affects how we feel. Be conscious on your vocabulary, and watch it shape your path. When we honour ourselves with good words, including praise for ourselves and others, we fuel our ability to live a good life.

Open your windows wide and often, and replace recycled air with a fresh Qi.

Invite guests over and feed them this indicates you are abundant enough to feed many mouths, you generate a prosperous energy and like energy attracts more like energy. This also enhances happiness in your space.

Appreciate the true abundance in your relationships and space. When you practice appreciation in your environment, all those who come into your space feel love. When you notice and show gratitude for what is good in your life, it amplifies a trail for more success to your life.

Change your home or workspace by giving it beauty and order, and it will fill with purpose and clarity. Life imitates our environments, show and act with love daily and the big things you desire manifest more easily. When positive experiences occur around you, give thanks. This is a sign that more good things are on their way.

Direct the flow of Qi with mirrors, lights, plants, colours, and items. Some obstacles are good, because they slow rushing Qi and enhance Feng Shui, however, some are bad, because they collect and spread stagnant Qi. Sense whether the obstacles feel good or bad. To direct the flow of energy down a hall to rooms such as the sleeping areas or workspace, hang a mirror or an image with reflective glass opposite the door to each room. When an obstacle blocks the flow of Qi, such as a plant, place a mirror so that it can reflect the energy toward thee direction you want the Qi to flow.

Keep things clean and organised.

The colour for love and romance is rose pink.

For intimate relationships place love symbols such as cupids, hearts and birds in pairs, as well as two chairs beside each other.

Cherry red on the bed cover enhances passion. Try to find something that works for both you and your partner. Place passionate images of you and your partner above the bed

Work together toward the same future.

When your friends or partner compliment you, thank them and let them know how happy it makes you.

Take regular holidays with your intimate partner, walk with them along the beach, do a meditation class or a retreat.

Go out dancing and celebrate.

Depending on your relationship goals, place a couple of love birds or a family of birds in the South area of your living room and workplace.

In your relationships, your task is to create harmony in your family, wherever they are.

Be spontaneous and creative with your intimate partner.

Take enough time to enjoy people.

To have a great relationship with yourself, take a meditation class or listen to a guided meditation

Be mindful of your boundaries. Help and mentor people but ensure you have boundaries, without them you will lose yourself in the relationship

See your partner or relationships as your greatest wealth and abundance.

Build strong bonds with your mother, loved ones and colleagues.

To avoid games and drama in your love life, avoid any kind of games, such as video games or board games, in the southwest.

Do not leave wastebaskets, clutter, or dirt in any direction that you activate.

Activate General Directions, in lounge room, workspace and bedrooms unless otherwise stated – pertaining the connected direction.

Do not place dried flowers, the positive Qi no longer exists in these.

Many have discovered the benefits of Feng Shui. If you would like to invite more success in your life with relationships and collaboration, begin with these principles and expand the energy in your home or workspace. In the eastern culture, those who find success through Feng Shui practises do not sell their homes once they become millionaires. They keep it for luck and continued good energy, even if they move into a new house.

Everything we do is controlled by the energy we put into it. Feng Shui helps release stagnated energy and escorts in good energy. Those who find the right balance in their homes discover that when the right energy is in place their success increases. Feng Shui is an ancient science and art that many people have had success with, and it's possible for you to have that same success, as well

For complete and comprehensive balancing, activations and cures for your home or workspace, contact a Feng Shui Consultant. Please note: Direction identification with a compass is the only way to get an accurate reading of your environment. More than half of the people who conduct their own Feng Shui compass readings do it incorrectly. It's imperative that it's accurate; creating analyses based on inaccurate readings is worse than doing nothing to correct or remedy inauspicious elements in your home.

Create a Vision board

A vision board is a paper or board where you put in the centre a recent image of yourself in a professional or enhancing outfit, depending on the type of relationships you desire, ensure the image reflects this and what it means to you. Place images around it that represent great relationships, images that make you happy, touch your feelings, of tenderness and collaboration. Place your vision board in the southeast direction in your workspace.

Chinese Proverb
If there is light in the soul, there will be beauty in the person.
If there is beauty in the person, there will be harmony in the house.
If there is harmony in the house, there will be order in the nation.
If there is order in the nation, there will be peace in the world.

Being Gracious and Appreciation

Being Gracious and feeling appreciation are powerful processes, and both invite a tremendous flow of positive Qi that continues to amplify as this is practiced daily. The next pages are simple lists of statements and things that help us feel good. Use these lists, choose your favourites, rewrite them, add to them, and play with them. Make this a daily occupation. Feel good now! And your abundance for health, success, relationships and growth will come swiftly.

99 Things You Can Be Gracious for on Any Given Day
I am gracious for…

1) Blazing orange and magenta sunsets
2) Quiet dawns in the darkness of early morning
3) Jacaranda trees
4) Exotic flowers like lilies and orchids
5) Books
6) Comfy, warm home on a cold day
7) Neon-green newborn grass emerging in spring
8) Supportive, loyal friends

9) Giving and receiving
10) Art in all its forms
11) Sparkles on the surface of water
12) Sturdy strong trees
13) Strong bodies that move us
14) Fairy lights
15) The first spring flower rising up
16) Optimism
17) Positivity
18) Silliness
19) Gratitude!
20) Indoor plumbing
21) Laughing till your tummy hurts
22) Deep emotion and passion
23) Our guides and angels
24) Turquoise
25) Walks in nature
26) A favorite song
27) Dancing madly
28) The golden light on nearby mountains
29) Doors for privacy
30) Quantum physics
31) Infinity

32) Worlds upon worlds
33) Feng Shui
34) A warm soup in winter
35) Clear deep rushing rivers
36) Jumpers and jackets
37) Baby lambs, puppies, kittens
38) Food glorious food
39) Too many bubbles in a bubble bath
40) My skin
41) Goofy faces
42) My happy family
43) Technology that connects the world
44) Pen and paper
45) Renoir, Picasso, Van Gogh
46) Pungent fragrances of lavender, rosemary, mint, rose
47) Pop Music to rock out to
48) Wisdom through the ages
49) Words like wonderful, luscious and nourish
50) Mother Teresa
51) Modern day mystics
52) Playtime especially when we are all grown up
53) Looking at the night sky
54) Comfortable bed
55) Unfurling of a fern frond

56) Water! Drinking it and knowing we are mostly made of it
57) The universal language of music
58) Yellow
59) Scurrying possums
60) The bustle and mix of animals, people, cars and bikes in Melbourne
61) Stretching our bodies
62) Hugs and kisses
63) Sharing with like-minded friends
64) The whole intricate, multi-layered systems of our bodies
65) Siblings through thick and thin
66) Loving, caring, nurturing mothers
67) Steady, sensible, hardworking fathers
68) Double rainbows
69) The wonder of birth!
70) Peace, quiet, serenity
71) Cars that transport us
72) The internet
73) The brilliant, bright extravaganza of summer
74) The vast ocean – the waves and tides and immensity
75) The magic of life
76) Scientists and mathematicians
77) Magenta

78) Routines we can count on
79) The fact that our world is spinning and we feel stable
80) Tropical islands
81) Dancing and laughing
82) Red
83) Melodious singers
84) The beat of drums
85) Enjoying a cool salad on a hot summer day
86) Honesty and forthrightness – people you can count on
87) Exquisite rain falling
88) Blue, and all the myriad of shades of it
89) Eyes that are a window to the soul
90) Smiles
91) Love – agape love, family love, self-love
92) The feeling of joy that upwells from within
93) The Earth's incredible beauty
94) Purple
95) Other life in the universe that is undoubtedly there
96) Particles and waves dancing and disappearing
97) Confidence and Trust
98) Kind deeds and compassion
99) All the things left off this list…

NATURAL JOYS

Think about these one at a time before going on to the next one.

1. Being in love.
2. Laughing so hard your face hurts.
3. A hot shower.
4. No queues at the supermarket.
5. Taking a drive on a pretty road.
6. Hearing your favourite song on the radio.
7. Lying in bed listening to the rain outside.
8. Hot towels fresh out of the dryer.
9. Chocolate milkshake ... or vanilla ... or strawberry!
10. A bubble bath.
11. Giggling.
12. A good conversation.
13. Finding a note in your jacket from last winter.
14. Running through sprinklers.
15. Laughing for absolutely no reason at all.
16. Having someone tell you that you're beautiful.
17. Accidentally overhearing someone say something nice about you.

18. Waking up and realising you still have a few hours left to sleep.

19. Making new friends or spending time with old ones.

20. Having someone play with your hair.

21. Sweet dreams.

22. Making eye contact with a cute stranger.

23. Holding hands with someone you care about.

24. Running into an old friend and realising that some things (good or bad) never change.

25. Watching the expression on someone's face as they open a much-desired present from you.

26. Getting out of bed every morning and being grateful for another beautiful day.

27. Knowing that somebody misses you.

28. Getting a hug from someone you care about deeply.

29. Knowing you've done the right thing, no matter what other people think.

For more information about this author
And other books:
www.terminaashton.com
www.terminafengshui.com
www.perpelflame.com
www.thehappymagnet.com

Termina Feng Shui

www.ingramcontent.com/pod-product-compliance
Lightning Source LLC
Chambersburg PA
CBHW050445010526
44118CB00013B/1681